A Weekly Guide for Two Network Partners Working through The 12-Week Workbook Study to a Proven Path to Sexual Integrity

JOEL HESCH

For more information or to order other books visit our website: www.ProvenMen.org

Published and printed in the U.S.A. by Goshen Press Lynchburg, VA.

Details in stories or anecdotes have been changed to protect the identities of the persons involved.

Interior Design
1106 Design

Cover Design
Prototype

Hesch, Joel

A Weekly Guide for Two Network Partners Working through The 12-Week Workbook Study to a Proven Path to Sexual Integrity

ISBN: 978-1-940011-14-1

1. Sex—Religious aspects—Christianity. 2. Temptation. 3. Christian men—Religious life. 4. Sexual Health Recover.

TABLE OF CONTENTS

Passionate for God,
Repentant in spirit,
Open and honest,
Victorious in living,
Eternal in perspective, and
Networking with other *Proven Men*.

Introduction

Congratulations! You've made an important decision by including a *network partner* on your journey. Having a true *network partner* gives you an opportunity to openly share your struggles and victories with someone who is going through the same thing. (If you haven't already read our article on our website regarding the importance and role of a *network partner,* plan to do so. It is attached as Appendix A, "Accountability is a Key to Breaking Free from the Grip of Lust".)

Each day you and your *network partner* will individually work through *The 12-Week Study to a Proven Path to Sexual Integrity,* then you'll meet every week to discuss with your *network partner* what you've learned and share your lives.

SET A WEEKLY TIME

Agree in advance with your *network partner* how long you will meet, both in terms of time and duration. We recommend that you commit to meet one hour a week for the 13 weeks it takes to have an initial meeting and work through the 12-Week Study. You're tackling an intense issue and it will require an intense commitment. Therefore, block out a set day and time during the week for the meeting and guard it. Be sure to also select a location where you can openly discuss sensitive topics.

THE FORMAT

Week 1 is the initial meeting and has a different format than future meetings. In that meeting you agree to certain ground rules, such as confidentiality, a commitment to being open, and meeting for 12 more weeks. You will spend 10 to 15 minutes each sharing your stories, including struggles with sexual integrity. There will also be a time for prayer. Basically, the first meeting is designed to get to know each other and set the stage work for networking and future meetings as you work through the 12-Week Study. For the first weekly meeting only, feel free to read the Guide prior to the meeting for Week 1 (and even to share in advance with your *network partner* the Guide for Week 1).

The formats for Weeks 2–13 will be based on a new but thereafter consistent format, beginning in prayer, sharing a feeling you had during the week, spending 5–10 minutes discussing your week, reviewing the weekly memory verse, answering suggested discussion questions, mentioning anything from the Study that week that struck you, and closing in prayer. We suggest that you not read the Guide in advance prior to those meetings. Rather, allow the meetings to unfold as you work through this Guide together. Simply bring the Guide with you to work through with your *network partner.*

Each weekly outline has more than enough material and discussion questions to last more than an hour. Therefore, you'll need to monitor the time. Don't feel rushed to get through everything. It's not about checking off homework, but engaging in heartwork that leads to change. Of course, feel free to tailor the meetings to each of your needs as *network partners.*

Finally, remember to bring this Guide, the 12-Week Study, and a Bible with you to each meeting.

Again, congratulations. You are now a permanent part of the fellowship of Proven Men. You can do this.

Plan to return to our website for additional resources, and refer others to it at www.ProvenMen.org.

Week 1

The Initial Meeting

Greet. Hug each other. (Yes, that's right, go ahead and hug each other. It may be uncomfortable, but start a practice of hugging each other when you greet, and again when you end each meeting. It breaks down barriers and sets the right tone for your new *networking* relationship.)

Prayer. Each man should pray. (Prayer is such an important component, that each of you should say a short prayer from your hearts. Be sure to pray for your *network partner.*)

Ground Rules and Confidentiality. Briefly discuss or mention that you both agree that what is said here stays here.

> **Raise Any Questions.** (If you have any questions about the meetings, or anything else, have the freedom to raise them. Perhaps something in the intro to the 12-Week Study raised a question for you. Feel free to talk about it now.)

Share Your Stories. Read the following Note before you share your stories:

> If each of you as *network partners* are going to be an encourager, you need to know where your partner is at and what he struggles with. Also, a weight is lifted once you share all of your secret sins. There is such freedom in confession of sins.
>
> Secrets are what keep us hiding. So plan to openly share. (If any unconfessed sins come to your mind later, then share it in this or a future meeting.) God wants to give you freedom. God is faithful to forgive each sin that we confess, so be sure to confess each one. Be sure

to share details, such as how often you use pornography, how often you masturbate, and details of other ways in which you struggle.

Right now, one should begin by sharing his story. Spend 10–15 minutes. Be vulnerable and openly share your struggles. Afterward, the other partner should affirm him, such as telling him you are proud of him and believe in him. (Follow the same process for the next man.)

PROVEN Acronym. Read the list of six essential elements of the "PROVEN" acronym:

Passionate for God,
Repentant in spirit,
Open and honest,
Victorious in living,
Eternal in perspective, and
Networking with other Proven Men.

Now commit to put each of them into practice each new day.

Optional: Comments about the Companion Book. If you read the companion Proven Men book *(A PROVEN Path to Sexual Integrity: Help with pornography, masturbation or other forms of sex addiction from a Biblical perspective)*, feel free to mention something that struck you and allow a short discussion.

Closing the Meeting. As you near the end of your time, both of you should take time to commit to contacting each other during the week. (Contacting each other is something you need to do each week, whether it is sending an encouraging text, email or telephone call. Don't wait for the other man to initiate contact, but be someone who reaches out one or more times each week. Don't underestimate the impact of a short text.)

Prayer. Both should pray. Say what is on your heart. Be sure to hug as you depart.

Week 

(based on Week One Study materials)

Greet & Prayer. Don't neglect to hug when you greet, and each man should pray.

Feelings Chart. Turn to *Appendix B* for the Feelings Chart, which is also located at *Appendix F* to the 12-Week Study. Share a feeling you have now or had during the week.

Check in. Spend 5–10 minutes each sharing how your week went. Share any struggles or setbacks. Share any victories.

Memory Verse. Both should recite (or read aloud) the memory verse.

> "'Teacher, which is the greatest commandment in the law?' Jesus replied, 'Love the Lord your God with all of your heart and with all of your soul and with all of your mind.' This is the first and greatest commandment. And the second is like it: 'Love your neighbor as yourself.'" (Matthew 22:36–39)
>
> Discuss how it impacted you and how to live it out.

Two Verses. Read aloud the following two passages.

- Colossians 2:20–23
- Matthew 12:43–45

Discussion: Discuss how these verses show you how they help in the battle for purity.

Afterward, read the following Note.

The first is a great statement demonstrating why neither programs nor the setting of boundaries stop temptation or bring lasting healing. The second is a wonderful analogy of why merely sweeping away access to bad inputs will not transform a heart and lead to permanent freedom. These verses drive home the point that the one way out of bondage to sin is in an intimate relationship with the One true Lord where we rely upon His strength.

More Verses. Read the following verses:

- Romans 2:8
- Psalm 119:36
- James 3:14–16
- Matthew 23:25
- Philippians 2:3

Discussion: Talk about how you felt or were impacted by one or more of these verses.

Afterward, read the following Note.

The goal of reading Scripture is to meet with God and to become transformed into the image of Christ. It's better to read and meditate on one verse with passion and repentance than to race through ten pages or read the Bible merely to check off homework.

The Study. Share what struck you from the Study.

Prayer. Before you go to the Lord in prayer, answer this question in your heart, "Do I want to be humble and repentant?" Now, each man should pray, with this thought or question in mind. As you pray, view it as a time to talk to God about this or making decisions and commitments, as well as a time of confession and repentance.

Homework. Contact each other during the week. Keep working through the Study each day and commit to meeting again next week. Be sure to share exciting truths with your wife, if married, and with others.

Special Note: The format for Weeks 3 through 13 will be very similar to this week. Be sure to bring your Guide, the Study, and a Bible.

Week 

(based on Week Two Study materials)

Greet & Prayer. Hug when you greet, and each man should pray.

Feelings Chart. Turn to *Appendix B.* Share a feeling you have now or had during the week.

Check in. Spend 5–10 minutes each sharing how your week went. Share struggles, setbacks, or victories.

Thought Life. Read the following Note:

> The goal of Proven Men is not merely to stop looking at pornography or masturbating, but to strive for absolute purity and a clean heart and mind. Sin begins in the mind, and when we allow impure thoughts to remain in our heads, it is just a matter of time before we act them out. Pay attention next week to your thought life and be willing to discuss it.
>
> Discussion: Now, each man should discuss any struggles you had with your thought life this week.

Memory Verse. Both should recite (or read aloud) the memory verse.

> "Finally, brothers, whatever is true, whatever is noble, whatever is right, whatever is pure, whatever is lovely, whatever is admirable—if anything is excellent or praiseworthy—think about such things." (Philippians 4:8)

Discussion: How does the memory verse address daydreams and fantasies?

Afterward, read the following Note.

Be mindful that all fantasies, not just sexual fantasies, are sinful. This includes dreaming about being a hero, saving the life of the President, winning the lottery, getting awards at work, or any other fantasy not based upon real life.

Discuss whether you agree that all fantasies are (or can be) sinful.

Afterward, read the following Note.

For many, it seems hard enough stopping sexual fantasies without concentrating upon all other fantasies, but that is important in winning the battle of controlling our thought lives. Fantasy is in the same category as coveting. It may reveal that we are not content or it may indicate that we are not trusting God. We might be dreaming of a life different from the one He gave us or that we want to be the center of attention and live an easy life. Therefore, we must guard our minds at all times about all things, including daydreams. Freedom from bondage to lust requires an across-the-board battle and commitment.

Right now, read 2 Corinthians 10:5.

Do you Want to Get Well? Turn to and read John 5:1–9.

Discussion: Answer the following questions:

- How long had he been at the well?
- Why do you think Jesus asked the man if he wanted to get well?
- When Jesus asked the man if he wanted to get well, what did he say?
- Why didn't Jesus address the response?
- What question did Jesus ask, and why?

Note: Often, a good question will prompt a person to make a good decision that changes the way he approaches life afterward. God wanted the man to finally address the root issues that kept him from trusting God.

- What did Jesus ask the man to do and what did it require?

  Note: Picking up a mat may not have seemed much like a healing path, but for a lame man, it certainly was; it required conviction, faith, and action. Notice the change in the man. He did not argue with Jesus. He was done making excuses. He could have said, "Are you crazy? I am lame. I cannot pick up my mat, let alone walk." Instead, he responded to the question by finally wanting to get well. He had conviction and was done living out the victim role. He wanted to be well. He also had faith. He didn't doubt that God could make Him walk. Finally, he acted upon his faith. He reached over to get the mat and tried to stand. Healing resulted when he followed God.

  The same is true for us. We must turn to the Lord with conviction, faith, and action to be healed from whatever wounds cause us to shrink into fantasy or turn to other selfish sexual conduct.

- Ask yourself, "Do I really want to get well? (Make that commitment now.)

- Ask yourself, "Am I willing to do whatever it takes?"

  Note: This is one of the most important decisions a man must make in order to live a Proven life. If anyone lacks this resolve, he will find that he keeps cycling between setbacks and making excuses for the next 38 years like the man at the well. It is vital to make a firm decision to be "willing to do whatever it takes," even if that means cutting out TV to allow time for the Study each day and for the other things you are learning about.

  It's time to end self-effort. Christ is asking each man to pick up the mat of conviction and realize that turning to the world is sinful, whether it involves pornography or any other sin. He is asking the men to put their faith in God, not in self-help programs. This means giving God complete control over their lives, including thought lives. He is asking them to act upon what they know God is leading them to do, whether it is filling their minds with godly inputs by doing the daily Study or cutting out sinful thoughts, such as second looks, dwelling on fantasy, or looking at pornography.

  Right now, make a firm decision that you will do whatever it takes to live out sexual integrity.

The Study. If time, share what struck you from the Study.

Prayer. Both should pray. Include in your closing prayer a commitment to wanting to get well, and being willing to do whatever it takes. (Be sure to hug as you depart.)

Homework. Contact each other during the week. In addition, ponder during the week the bold statement that all fantasies, not just sexual ones, are sin. Purpose to start recognizing what you dwell upon during the week and to keep notes. Set a bouncer at the door to take captive all thoughts and make them conform to Christ.

Week 

(based on Week Three Study materials)

Greet & Prayer. Hug when you greet, and each man should pray.

Feelings Chart. Turn to *Appendix B*. Share a feeling.

Check in. Spend 5–10 minutes each sharing how your week went.

Memory Verse. Both should recite (or read aloud) the memory verse:

> "I have been crucified with Christ and I no longer live, but Christ lives in me. The life I live in the body, I live by faith in the Son of God, who loved me and gave Himself for me." (Galatians 2:20)
>
> Discussion: State how you were impacted by this verse, and how you plan to live it out in practical terms.

The Shovel. At Week 3, Day 4 of the Study, we provided a word picture of a shovel that represents man's self-efforts. Discuss what is meant by: "the shovel of self-effort." Next discuss how self-efforts and performance based living interfere with living out a Proven Life.

Additional discussion questions:

- How do you try to control your life?
- What prevents you from putting the shovel down?

Gift. Read these verses:

- John 6:37
- John 10:28
- Luke 15:10

Afterward, read the following Note.

Picture right now that God the Father is telling you that you are a gift He is giving to Jesus. That's right, "You are a gift from God the Father to Jesus."

That's how Christ sees each of you. He treasures you personally. He loves you. It is time to believe God over Satan. It is time to put God's promises in our hearts and into action! God's grace will change you if you yield to Him. (Start believing God. You don't need to prove your worth to Christ because He sees you as a present that God the Father gave Him, and He will treasure you and protect you and build you up. He will never trade you in or stop loving you, no matter what!)

- What struck you from the verses or the Note?

God Is Good. Refer to Week 4, Day 3 in the Proven Men Study, where you were asked if you truly believe that God is good and were asked to put two big stars there if you could not. Ask yourself these questions:

- What struggle do I have with seeing God as good?

- What area of my life am I holding onto or not opening up to God?

Forgiveness. Read the following verses on forgiveness:

- Ephesians 1:7
- Colossians 1:13–14
- 1 John 1:9

- What struck you?

Note: Be willing to accept God's forgiveness. Believe it. Don't try to earn it.

The Study. Share what struck you from the Study.

Prayer. A suggested way to pray this week is what is referred to as "pray read" from the Bible. Turn to Colossians 1:9–12. Replace your *network partner's* name for any nouns and pronouns such as "I," "us," or "we." You can also modify the passage slightly to make it more personal and real. For instance, say, "Blessed is Tim because he walks according to the law of the Lord. Oh Father, please have mercy on my brother Tim and cause Tim to walk according to your law. Blessed is Tim because he keeps your statutes, and Tim seeks you with all of his heart." Take turns and both of you should pray read these four verses.

Be sure to hug as you depart.

Homework. Contact each other during the week. Consider sharing next week a Psalm or letter you are encouraged to write to the Lord.

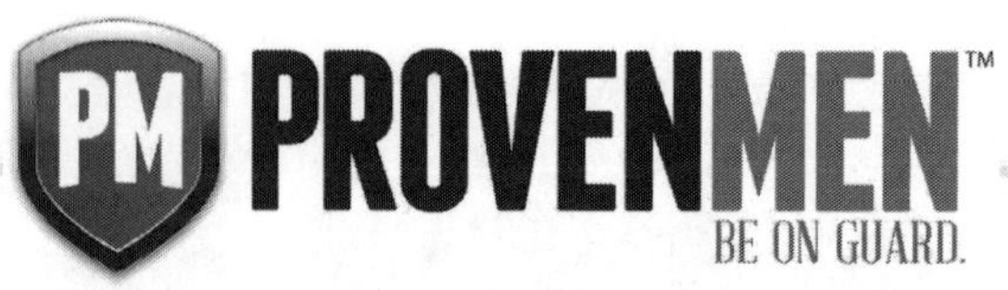

Passionate for God,
Repentant in spirit,
Open and honest,
Victorious in living,
Eternal in perspective, and
Networking with other *Proven Men*.

Week

(based on Week Four Study materials)

Greet & Prayer. Hug when you greet, and each man should pray.

Feelings Chart. Turn to *Appendix B.* Share a feeling.

Check in. Spend 5–10 minutes each sharing how your week went.

Setbacks. Spend a few more minutes sharing any setbacks.

Afterward, read the following Note.

Week 4 in the Study addresses setbacks because the honeymoon period is likely over. Those who have previously gone through the Study share a common experience. At first, they enjoy some instant freedom after joining a support group or networking, but now life's pressures are knocking at the door, and many experience some setbacks. If that description fits you, you are not defective or unique. It is like first riding a bike; as you are learning how, you will fall at times.

Victory. Victory is not the absence of sin in a life, but how you respond by repenting. Victory is the process of transforming your heart and cultivating a desire to be intimate with the Lord.

Life Verse. Read aloud Romans 8:1.

Read this Note:

Some of you need to make this your life verse. In reaction to a setback, many men condemn themselves and view themselves as being unworthy of God's grace or love or forgiveness. This is backward thinking. God proved His love by dying on the cross. God also tells us that there is now no condemnation for those who seek after Him. We need to believe God at His word. You may have to read this verse dozens of times, memorize it, and commit to believing that you have no right to condemn yourself or to live a defeated life. God lives in you, and forgives you, so you must accept His forgiveness. Your reaction to grace should not be to try to earn it, but to love Him back. It is that simple. Instead of beating yourself up when you stumble, you must purpose to draw closer to God.

Mark this passage in your Bible. Consider making it one of you life verses.

Memory Verse. Both should recite (or read aloud) the memory verse and state its impact on you.

"Therefore, get rid of all moral filth and the evil that is so prevalent and humbly accept the word planted in you, which can save you. Do not merely listen to the word, and so deceive yourselves. Do what it says." (James 1:21–22)

The Sword. God created men with a natural desire to impact the world. That's why it is so hard to put down the shovel of self-effort. You were born to accomplish tasks. The good news is that there are some actions involved in living out a Proven life, despite not striving to control life.

Consider this this word picture:

Assume you're huddled in a cave. It's dark and misty. Outside are fierce dragons. You hear their high-pitched screeches and the eerie screams of their victims. You're stricken with fear. Yet you know that if you stay hidden in the cave, others who need your help will be killed. A bright light suddenly appears as a mighty warrior clad in golden armor and a sharp sword enters. He looks you in the eyes and says,

I am the King of Kings, Prince of Peace, Deliverer, Master, and Redeemer. I am entering into battle with the dragons. I invite you to join me. I have everything you need to be victorious. I have a suit of armor specially designed for you. The dragons cannot penetrate your armor. You cannot suffer a life-threatening blow or injury. I also have a sword for you more powerful than their weapons. Here is my promise to you. Victory is assured if you simply wear your armor, use the sword, and follow me. Will you go with me?

This is a dream come true. Who wouldn't want to join that battle? You're guaranteed victory. You're assured you won't suffer a mortal wound. Yes, you may suffer some minor scrapes and bruises, but you are slaying dragons ... you are saving the princess! You're living large—the way God designed it for you. And, when you get to heaven, you will even get a new, heavenly body.

Confirm that you will join with God and pick up His sword and fight alongside other Proven Men. If you are reluctant, discuss this now. Include in your discussion if you are afraid to trust God.

Share a Psalm. If time, read aloud a Psalm you wrote. Otherwise, email it to each other.

The Study. If time, share what struck you from the Study.

Prayer. Use a popcorn style of prayer, as shown in the Note below.

Popcorn prayer consists of praying short prayers and jumping in. One man prays one short prayer or praise. Keep it to one topic and even one sentence. Then the other man prays one sentence. Go back and forth or jump in.

Homework. Contact each other during the week. Start preparing game plans for tempting situations. (If you don't have a game plan, you will resort to prior ways of acting.)

Be sure to hug as you depart.

(Use this style of popcorn praying with your wife, if married, or other men in other settings.)

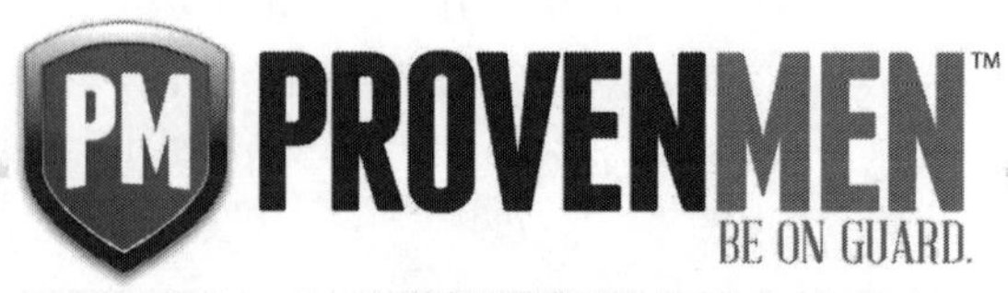

Passionate for God,
Repentant in spirit,
Open and honest,
Victorious in living,
Eternal in perspective, and
Networking with other *Proven Men*.

Week 

(based on Week Five Study materials)

Greet & Prayer. Hug when you greet, and each man should pray.

Feelings Chart. Turn to *Appendix B.* Share a feeling.

Check in. Spend 5–10 minutes each sharing how your week went.

Memory Verse. Both should recite (or read aloud) the memory verse and state its impact on you.

> "Be joyful always; pray continually; give thanks in all circumstances, for this is God's will for you in Christ Jesus." (1 Thessalonians 5:16–18)

View of Your Dad. Spend 5–10 minutes each describing and discussing your relationship with your dad.

> Afterward, read the following Note.
>
> Many men find it hard to see God the Father as good, loving, and forgiving because their own dads were not these things.
>
> Now, discuss if and how your relationship with your dad affects your view of God. (Plan to use this discussion to help move past the pain of the relationship with your father or father figure and turn to and trust God.)

Optional: If you have additional time left, go over any discussion topics that you did not get to from last week or share what struck you from the Study.

Prayer. Both should pray. (If you meet in a non-public place, kneel during the prayer time.)

Be sure to hug as you depart.

Homework. Contact each other during the week. Keep sharing exciting truths you are learning with others. Consider creating special times to meet with the Lord, such as prayer walks, meditating on the attributes of God, and writing notes to God.

> Note: For married men, regularly sharing with your wives what you are learning in the Study and in meetings with your *network partner* will greatly encourage and strengthen your spouse and help rebuild trust. Wives will see that this time is different from all the other times you may have said you would try to stop or change.

Week 7

(based on Week Six Study materials)

Greet & Prayer. Hug when you greet, and each man should pray.

Feelings Chart. Turn to *Appendix B.* Share a feeling.

Check in. Spend 5–10 minutes each sharing how your week went.

Memory Verse. Both should recite (or read aloud) the memory verse and state its impact on you.

> "Therefore, I urge you, brothers, in view of God's mercy, to offer your bodies as living sacrifices, holy and pleasing to God—this is your spiritual act of worship. Do not conform any longer to the pattern of this world, but be transformed by the renewing of your mind. Then you will be able to test and approve what God's will is—His good, pleasing and perfect will." (Romans 12:1–2)

Names God Has For You. In the Study at Week 6, Day 3, we listed the names God has for you to strengthen your faith and keep you from doubting God's love for you and willingness t o give you His strength as you face trials and temptations in life. Below is the same list. Take turns reading aloud each of these names. As you do, start believing in and trusting in God's love for you and commit to live out your names and position in Christ:

- **Royal Priest** (1 Peter 2:9)
- **God's Holy People** (Ephesians 5:3)
- **Wonderfully Created** (Psalm 139:14)
- **Brother to Jesus** (Hebrews 2:11)
- **God's Possession** (Ephesians 1:14)

- **Dearly Loved** (Ephesians 5:1)
- **Adopted Son of God** (Ephesians 1:4)
- **Image of God** (Genesis 1:27)
- **Chosen by God** (Colossians 3:12)
- **Future Judge of Angels** (1 Corinthians 6:3)
- **God's Heir** (Galatians 4:7)
- **Ambassador of Christ** (2 Corinthians 5:20)
- **Friend of Jesus** (John 15:14–15)
- **Saint** (Psalm 34:9; 85:8)
- **Child of God** (1 John 3:1)
- **Salt and Light of the World** (Matthew 5:13–14)
- **Righteousness of God** (2 Corinthians 5:21)
- **New Creation** (2 Corinthians 5:17)
- **God's Workmanship** (Ephesians 2:10)
- **Temple of the Holy Spirit** (1 Corinthians 6:19)
- **Member of God's Household** (Ephesians 2:19)
- **Citizen of Heaven** (Philippians 3:20).

Afterward read the following Note.

Many men are stricken with guilt, shame, and feelings of unworthiness. This is a common trap set by the devil in an attempt to keep Christians from approaching God as a friend, seeing Him as good, and trusting Him with all areas of their lives. It is time to use God's truth to defeat the lies men have heard throughout their lives.

These are the names God uses for you. The King of the Universe, our Creator, calls you by these names, so you have the opportunity to embrace them and stop listening to the lies of Satan or others who call us other names. This is the truth, so you can believe it! Start believing God loves you deeply and unconditionally.

Do This and You'll Never Fall. Men want a list of things to do. Turn to 2 Peter 1:5–10 for a list of eight things you must do to never fall.

Discuss how hard it will be to do all of them.

Now turn to and read 2 Peter 1:3–4.

Discuss how this passage relates to the list of eight rules you are to keep.

(Be sure to grasp the good news that it is God who gives you what you need to live pure and not to fall. Discuss how men tend to be performance-based (and sometimes even legalistic), and how this can keep us from accepting God's grace.)

Now turn to and read Galatians 5:16.

What is the key to keeping from stumbling?

Discuss what it looks like in practice to live by God's Spirit and to put into place each day all six elements of the PROVEN acronym.

The Study. If time, share what struck you from the Study.

Prayer. Both should pray. Say what is on your heart. Be sure to hug as you depart.

Homework. Contact each other during the week. Consider setting aside five minutes this week where you are still and ask God this question: "God, what is holding me back from seeking deep intimacy with You and turning over all aspects of my life to You? Please reveal it to me and give me Your strength to break free."

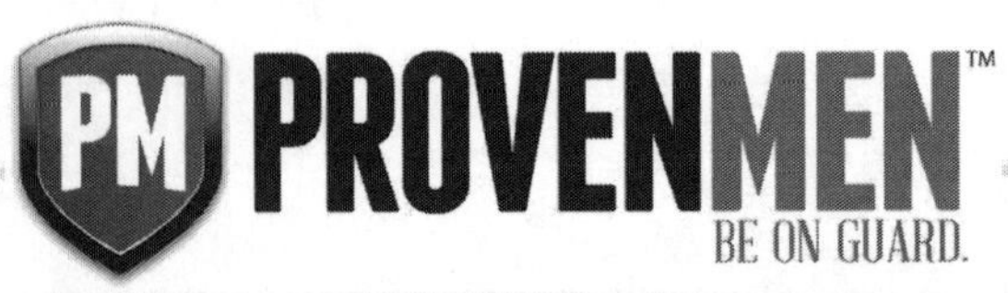

Passionate for God,
Repentant in spirit,
Open and honest,
Victorious in living,
Eternal in perspective, and
Networking with other *Proven Men*.

Week 

(based on Week Seven Study materials)

Greet & Prayer. Hug when you greet, and each man should pray.

Feelings Chart. Turn to *Appendix B.* Share a feeling.

Check in. Spend 5–10 minutes each sharing how your week went.

Memory Verse. Both should recite (or read aloud) the memory verse and state its impact on you.

> "My dear brothers, take note of this: Everyone should be quick to listen, slow to speak and slow to become angry, for man's anger does not bring about the righteous life that God desires." (James 1:19–20)

Childhood Abuse. This week's Study included a discussion regarding childhood abuse. Don't gloss over this, but be willing to discuss any childhood abuse you suffered. Before you do, read the Note to set up the discussion.

> One major way in which many men are wronged is some form of childhood abuse (emotional, physical, or sexual). Sexual abuse is not limited to forced intercourse, and it can take many forms, including being exposed to pornography or naked adults, being shown how to masturbate, being touched by another person in an uncomfortable manner, receiving numerous enemas, or being teased about physical appearance and body image. Emotional abuse includes shame-based criticism, the withholding of love, and the prohibition of expressing feelings. For instance, a man's dad may never have hugged him or told him that he loved him.

It is often helpful to address the childhood abuse issue and see if it is a factor in why you shy away from relationships. When a person, and especially a child, is hurt or abused, it can be very destructive, and the effects very often carry over into adulthood. Abuse contributes to:

(1) walls being built around a person's heart

(2) a tendency to shy away from vulnerable and intimate relationships

(3) unhealthy styles of interaction with people

(4) hidden anger

When a man refuses to allow himself feelings or he experiences numbness, there is a good chance that he has been scarred in this way. Abuse may have led to shame, guilt, self-condemnation, and anger deep within the man's soul. Therefore, he withdraws from close relationships, the place where he could be wounded again. A man who has been wounded in this way also often retreats from God, and distance from God always causes us to take on the character of the world, which is filled with anger and is judgmental and selfish.

Discussion: Now, take turns describing any childhood abuse. (Be sure to affirm your *network partner.*)

Discuss any other childhood events that contribute to why it is hard for you to be open or to share your feelings, hopes or dreams with others.

The Study. If time, share what struck you from the Study.

Prayer. Both should pray. Be sure to hug as you depart.

Homework. Contact each other during the week. Next week the Study calls for a fast at lunch-time, if you are able. Consider skipping lunch next week and replacing that time with Bible reading and prayer.

Week 

(based on Week Eight Study materials)

Greet & Prayer. Hug when you greet, and each man should pray.

Feelings Chart. Turn to *Appendix B*. Share a feeling.

Check in. Spend 5–10 minutes each sharing how your week went.

Memory Verse. Both should recite (or read aloud) the memory verse and state its impact on you.

> "Godly sorrow brings repentance that leads to salvation and leaves no regret, but worldly sorrow brings death." (2 Corinthians 7:10)

Fasting. Read this Note:

The purposes of a fast:

(1) a spiritual preparation to meet with God by creating a focused time of reflection, dependence, and worship;

(2) a reminder to die to the basic principles of the world; and

(3) a discipline showing that life is more than eating.

Also remember that a fast is not a ritual that brings about God's favor. The Lord desires a humble heart that is fully devoted to Him and longs to meet with Him. God does not want sacrifice, but a merciful heart, as He says in Matthew 9:13: "God desires mercy, not sacrifice."

Now, turn to Matthew 6:17–18. After reading it, describe any experiences with fasting this week, and discuss how you think fasting is relevant to seeking godly sorrow and repentance.

Psalm 51. Psalm 51 is a call to repentance. Read it now.

If you wrote out your own Psalm 51 to the Lord, plan to share it now. (Otherwise, write one this week and send it by email to your *network partner.*)

Repentance. A person who is given over to a particular sin changes only when his heart toward God changes. Repentance also includes change.

Discuss how you have recently repented.

Next, discuss areas you still need to repent.

The Study. If time, share what struck you from the Study.

Prayer. Both should pray from your heart. Be sure to hug as you depart.

Homework. Contact each other during the week. Consider buying or renting the movie, *The Passion of the Christ*, because the next meeting calls for playing a portion of the movie. Thus, at the next meeting, you will need to find and play a five-minute portion where Jesus is beaten with whips very harshly. (These scene may also be available on the Internet.)

Week 10

(based on Week Nine Study materials)

Greet & Prayer. Hug when you greet, and each man should pray.

Feelings Chart. Turn to *Appendix B*. Share a feeling.

Check in. Spend 5–10 minutes each sharing how your week went.

Memory Verse. Both should recite (or read aloud) the memory verse and state its impact on you.

> "We demolish arguments and every pretension that sets itself up against the knowledge of God, and we take captive every thought to make it obedient to Christ." (2 Corinthians 10:5)

Discussion:

What thoughts did you have this week that you needed to be taken captive and did you take them captive right away?

Afterward, read the following Note.

There are 3 Rs for addressing temptations: RECOGNIZE, RUIN, and REPLACE. First, train yourself to recognize when your mind wanders or lusts. Second, ruin any impure thought. Don't let it linger. Set a bouncer in your mind to take captive and eradicate all lustful thoughts. Third, replace the thought with something pure or admirable. If you neglect to replace the thoughts, you are only engaging in human behavior modification techniques. The replacement aspect is a key component of the spiritual war game plan.

Now, describe in you own words what it looks like in practice to take every thought captive, and how you plan to do just that.

Movie Clip. Play the clip from the movie, *The Passion of the Christ*. (Play the scene where Jesus was being beaten by the soldiers. Stop after about 5 minutes.)

What was your reaction to this, and how are you feeling right now?

Why did Jesus have to suffer?

What is your response to that great love Jesus demonstrated for you?

The Study. Share what struck you from the Study.

Prayer. Both should pray. Be sure to hug as you depart.

Homework. Contact each other during the week. Plan to set aside five minutes this week to hear from the Lord as to what areas in your life you are still controlling.

The Details:

(1) Still your heart and find a quiet place to meet with the Lord, preparing yourself for asking Him to reveal what areas you are still controlling or refusing to turn over to Him.

(2) With a blank sheet of paper (or in your journal), earnestly ask God: “What am I holding onto?”

(3) Simply jot down any rough thoughts or flashes as they enter your mind. Do not dwell on any one item at this time, but just keep jotting down a word or two at a time. Keep asking the Lord if there is any other area, and simply write down anything that enters your mind.

(4) After several minutes of asking and seeking the Lord, go back to the sheet and read what you wrote down. Now ask the Lord to open your heart as you read each item. God will make it clear to you whether they were your own thoughts or Him speaking to you.

(5) Review the points about which you believe God was speaking to you. Ask Him to reveal more of how you have been holding onto these areas or acting in pride or selfishness. Talk to Him about it.

(6) Decide that you will respond and do whatever the Lord is asking you. Commit to act upon what God reveals to you. Don't hold back or fight the Holy Spirit by glossing over an item.

(7) Prepare a plan for acting. (Be a doer, not just a hearer —James 1:22.)

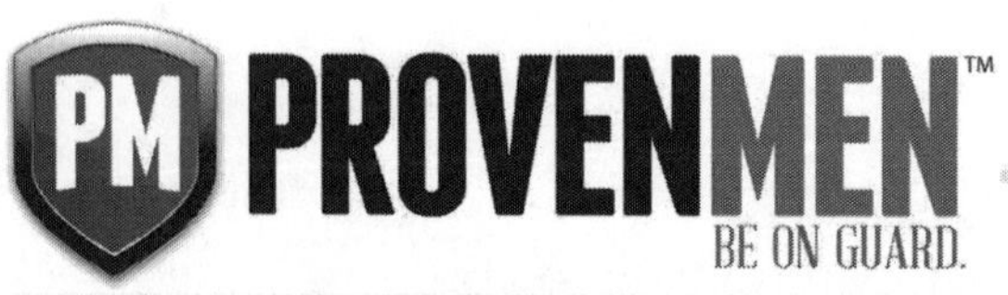

Passionate for God,
Repentant in spirit,
Open and honest,
Victorious in living,
Eternal in perspective, and
Networking with other *Proven Men*.

Week 

(based on Week Ten Study materials)

Greet & Prayer. Hug when you greet, and each man should pray.

Feelings Chart. Turn to *Appendix B.* Share a feeling.

Check in. Spend 5–10 minutes each sharing how your week went.

Holding Back? Discuss how well you are doing at making a daily decision for absolute purity.

Next, describe what you might be still holding onto, or what is holding you back.

Two Keys. Review this concept together:

There are two keys to breaking free from sexual sin:
(1) No longer considering turning to a certain sin as an option, and
(2) Being willing to do whatever it takes to be set free from that sin.

These two things will make all the difference in winning or losing the spiritual battle.

Discuss whether you made the firm decision that your particular sexual sin is no longer an option and you are willing to do whatever it takes. (Be sure to state in you own words what this means, how it helps in the battle, and what you plan to do to include these principles into your daily life.)

Memory Verse. Both should recite (or read aloud) the memory verse and state its impact on you.

> "Keep your lives free from the love of money and be content with what you have, because God has said, 'Never will I leave you; never will I forsake you.'" (Hebrews 13:5)

Next Study? There are only two more weeks in the Study. Discuss whether you plan to continue to meet weekly after these thirteen weeks end.

The Study. If time, share what struck you from the Study.

Prayer. Before you pray, open to Galatians 2:20. For prayer time, one man should first read this verse aloud and then pray based on this verse. Then, the next man should read the verse aloud and pray based on the verse.

Be sure to hug as you depart.

Homework. Contact each other during the week. Meditate on Galatians 2:20 throughout the coming week. Consider committing to journaling about it. Start deciding on what book you might want to work through together, such as a book on prayer or some other book suggested in *Appendix M* to the Study. You may need to order the book soon so it's here on time.

Week 

(based on Week Eleven Study materials)

Greet & Prayer. Hug when you greet, and each man should pray.

Feelings Chart. Turn to *Appendix B*. Share a feeling.

Check in. Spend 5–10 minutes each sharing how your week went.

Memory Verse. Both should recite (or read aloud) the memory verse and state its impact on you.

> "Be completely humble and gentle; be patient, bearing with one another in love." (Ephesians 4:2)

Verses. Read aloud the following verses:

- 1 Peter 5:6
- James 4:6
- Psalm 36:2
- Matthew 11:29–30

Discuss what impacted you from these verses.

Read Philippians 2:3.

Why does God want you to consider others more important than ourselves, and how do you do that?

What is the practical side of taking the focus off yourself?

Do you find it hard to give others compliments? (Explain why.)

Next Study? There is only one more week in the Study. Commit to continue to meet weekly. Pick out a book you want to meet weekly to discuss, and review one or two chapters per week. (Some suggestions are in *Appendix M* to the Study.) Order or buy it this week.

The Study. If time, share what struck you from the Study.

Prayer. Both should pray. Be sure to hug as you depart.

Homework. Contact each other during the week. Plan to give other men compliments this week, including co-workers. Don't shrug this off, but make the effort to give other men compliments this week. (This is a good antidote to your pride. It also helps you foster being open and encouraging others.)

Week 

(based on Week Twelve Study materials)

Greet & Prayer. Hug when you greet, and each man should pray.

Feelings Chart. Turn to *Appendix B.* Share a feeling.

Check in. Spend 5–10 minutes each sharing how your week went.

Memory Verse. Both should recite (or read aloud) the memory verse and state its impact on you.

> "But among you there must not be even a hint of sexual immorality, or of any kind of impurity, or of greed, because these are improper for God's holy people." (Ephesians 5:3)

Recap. Describe what impacted you the most from the thirteen weeks of meeting together.

Lifetime Process. Discuss how healing from sexual sin and living out a Proven life are lifetime processes.

> Read this Note:
>
> We will always be growing and persevering. Freedom is not a one-time or 12-week event. We must take on an eternal perspective and start viewing each temptation as an opportunity to honor God and to grow.

Setbacks. Discuss what it means that *the mark of a Proven Man is not the absence of sin, but how you respond to a setback.*

Afterward, read the following Note.

When you have a setback, don't throw in the towel or quit. Even a setback is an opportunity to grow and please God. It can make you humble and allow you to see yourself as you are: a needy, dependent servant. That is what pleases God. Otherwise, you become self-reliant and selfish, having no room or need for a close relationship with God. Also, if you have a setback, don't listen to the voice and lies of the devil. He will want you to feel so much shame that you don't go to God to receive the healing and forgiveness that the Lord loves to give.

If you don't feel like a spiritual giant, that's okay. In fact, it's good. When we think we are standing tall, we will fall. Besides, because healing and victory are lifetime processes, we can't expect to be spiritual giants in twelve weeks. The key point is that we keep putting on the armor of God each day, turning to and relying upon Him. It is important to measure each day of our lives by the Word of God, and the six elements of the PROVEN acronym are a great guideline.

P is for Passionate for God
R is for Repentant in Spirit
O is for Open and Honest
V is for Victorious in Living
E is for Eternal in Perspective, and
N is for Networked with other *Proven Men*

(Plan to memorize the acronym and to regularly test your life by it.)

Game Plan. Describe your game plan or how you will respond if you have a setback.

Comfort Others. At Week 12, Day 1 of the Study, we provided a word picture of the Dead Sea. It is lifeless and dead because, unlike all other seas, it is fed by many inlets but has no outlets. Therefore, all of the impurities remain in it, and it kills life. Discuss how the Dead Sea helps you see how *networking* and serving others is part of the antidote to sexual sin.

Afterward, read the following Note.

When you try to close your life off to others and hold onto the blessings of God, you harden your heart, and it turns hard or bitter. The antidote is to serve others and allow the spirit of God to flow through you into the lives of others.

Verse. Read aloud 2 Corinthians 1:3–5.

- Why does God comfort us?

- Describe ways in which you plan to use your struggles and even failures to build others up.

The Study. If time, share what struck you from the Study.

Prayer. Both should pray. Be sure to hug as you depart.

Homework. Be sure you have a game plan for networking with other Proven Men. If this season is over with this *network partner*, purpose to find another to keep networking with each week. In addition, consider becoming a Proven Men small group leader or go through the Study with another man who needs it. There are so many men that need a *network partner*. Plan to review the website: www.ProvenMen.org.

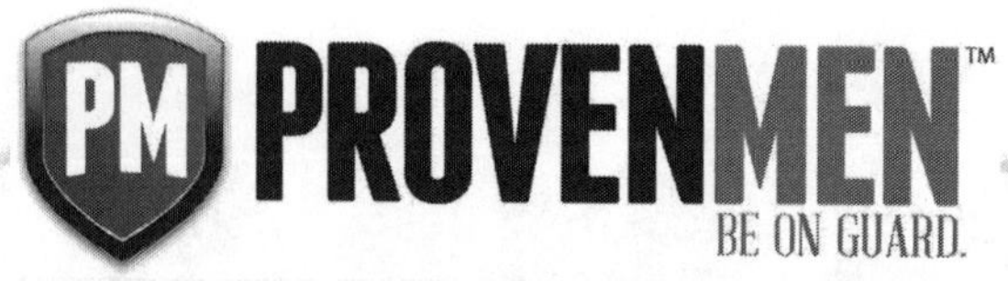

Passionate for God,
Repentant in spirit,
Open and honest,
Victorious in living,
Eternal in perspective, and
Networking with other *Proven Men*.

Appendix 

Accountability is a Key to Breaking Free from the Grip of Lust

Fighting to overcome lust, masturbation, pornography or other sexually compulsive activities is one of the hardest struggles most men will face in life. Yet, at times, it can seem like you're the only one in the battle. It also can be very frustrating to keep having setbacks. Perhaps you feel defeated because you've read self-help books teaching you techniques for fleeing from temptations or instructing you what to do after you stumble, but they never seem to bring lasting relief. You keep asking yourself,

Why doesn't it work for me?

Why am I still in bondage to sin?

The one thing missing from a self-directed healing path is accountability. Just how important is this? Well, no serious athlete attempts to compete without a coach, no successful business lacks managers, and no lasting government exists without layers of accountability. So why should a man expect to win a battle against sin all by himself—especially when it's a sin he has yet to overcome on his own after years of trying? Let's face it; we all need accountability. But we also need support and encouragement. When you wrap these together, we call it a *network partner*. In fact, God designed you to be connected to others in such a manner that lasting freedom normally won't work unless you walk the road to victory together with a *network partner*.

What holds you back from asking another man to be your *network partner*? Perhaps pangs of shame, guilt, and self-condemnation strike fear in your heart at the thought of openly sharing your failures and struggles. Maybe your pride and stubbornness won't let you admit you need help. Whatever your particular reason for shying away from including another man in your journey, remember that one of the largest barriers to experiencing lasting freedom is a refusal to link up with another man in a true *networking partnership*.

■ DEFINING TERMS

At its core, accountability means being obligated to account for your actions or being responsible to another. Perhaps this makes you bristle or want to run and hide. But, if you're willing to do things God's way—or if, perhaps, you're finally desperate enough to change—you'll be glad to hear the good news. God offers you a plan for true acceptance in a *networking partner*, instead of a blaming, shame-based form of accountability.

Although few Christian men quibble over whether they're accountable to God, those trapped in bondage to sexual sin often balk at God's proclamation that His children must also be accountable to and networked with another. The solution for addressing reoccurring setbacks is not to try harder by your own power, but to relinquish the stubborn pride that keeps you from surrendering your will to Christ by refusing to obey His command to *network* with other men.

If you've read our companion book, *A Proven Path to Sexual Integrity*, then you know that selfishness and pride are the real root issues behind this resistance. This same pride that makes you want to fight the battle on your own also feeds your selfish indulgence in forbidden sensual pleasures. It's time to embrace the Proven Path and take a *network partner*.

■ BIBLICAL NETWORK PARTNERSHIPS

Networking isn't synonymous with accountability, *per se*. Most accountability partners merely ask each other to admit whether or not they have sinned during the week. It can be very draining to meet weekly with someone simply to tell them you messed up. That's why that kind of accountability is short-lived. The experience is so miserable that it inadvertently encourages men to shade the truth, skirt the issue, or—let's be honest—outright lie.

Shame and ridicule are counterproductive. When you're already struggling with your commitment to change, what you really need is encouragement from another man who understands what it means to struggle with an issue like this.

PROVEN *network partnerships* are different. They aren't focused on catching each other in sin or calling a man out. They center on investing in each other's lives and having (perhaps for the first time) deep, intentional relationships. The Bible paints a vivid picture of the partnering relationship God designed for men that develops through *networking* within the brotherhood of believers. Consider the following ways the Lord says you are to *network* with other believers:

- **Helping:** "A brother is born for a time of adversity" *(Proverbs 17:17)*
- **Instructing:** We are each "competent to instruct one another" *(Romans 15:14)*
- **Comforting:** "Comfort those in any trouble with the comfort we ourselves receive from God" *(2 Corinthians 1:3–5)*
- **Serving:** "You, my brothers and sisters, were called to be free. But do not use your freedom to indulge the flesh; rather, serve one another humbly in love." *(Galatians 5:13)*
- **Restoring:** "Brothers and sisters, if someone is caught in a sin, you who live by the Spirit should restore that person gently. But watch yourselves, or you also may be tempted." *(Galatians 6:1)*
- **Carrying Burdens:** "Carry each other's burdens, and in this way you will fulfill the law of Christ" *(Galatians 6:2)*
- **Speaking Truth:** "Speaking the truth in love, we will grow to become in every respect the mature body of Him who is the head, that is, Christ" *(Ephesians 4:15)*
- **Teaching & Admonishing:** "Let the message of Christ dwell among you richly as you teach and admonish one another with all wisdom through psalms, hymns, and songs from the Spirit, singing to God with gratitude in your hearts" *(Colossians 3:16)*
- **Building Up:** "Build each other up" *(1 Thessalonians 5:11)*
- **Correcting:** "Correct, rebuke and encourage—with great patience and careful instruction *(2 Timothy 4:2)*
- **Encouraging:** "Encourage one another daily, as long as it is called 'Today,' so that none of you may be hardened by sin's deceitfulness" *(Hebrews 3:13)*
- **Spurring On:** "Let us consider how we may spur one another on toward love and good deeds" *(Hebrews 10:24)*
- **Meeting Together:** "Not giving up meeting together, as some are in the habit of doing, but encouraging one another" *(Hebrews 10:25)*
- **Confessing:** "Confess your sins to each other and pray for each other so that you may be healed" *(James 5:16)*

You may notice that we put "confessing" at the end of the list. The reason we did this is because most men equate accountability solely with a weekly meeting to confess their failures. That's not "networking." In fact, as you examine the context around this confessing verse, you'll notice that confessing is hinged on prayer and healing. Those don't happen simply by telling another that you had a setback. Rather, confessing is designed to mutually encourage, help, serve, build up, spur on, and warn of dangers.

As you accept God's command to and need for networking, you'll find that you'll grow in even more spiritual roles in aiding others—those who need your help as much as you need theirs. Here are a few more roles of *network partners:*

- **Keeping Confidences:** "A gossip separates close friends" *(Proverbs 16:28; 17:9)*
- **Warning to Flee:** "Flee from idolatry" *(1 Corinthians 10:14);* "flee the evil desires of youth and pursue righteousness, faith, love and peace, along with those who call on the Lord out of a pure heart" *(2 Timothy 2:22);* "flee from sexual immorality" *(1 Corinthians 6:18)*
- **Encouraging Purity:** "But among you there must not be even a hint of sexual immorality, or of any kind of impurity, or of greed, because these are improper for God's holy people" *(Ephesians 5:3);* "It is God's will that you should be sanctified: that you should avoid sexual immorality" *(1 Thessalonians 4:3)*
- **Inspiring to Stand Firm:** "Therefore, my brothers and sisters . . . stand firm in the Lord" *(Philippians 4:1);* "You ought to live holy and godly lives as you look forward to the day of God and speed its coming" *(2 Peter 3:11–12)*
- **Warning against being Idle or Disruptive:** "We urge you, brothers and sisters, warn those who are idle and disruptive, encourage the disheartened, help the weak, be patient with everyone" *(1 Thessalonians 5:14)*
- **Urging to Abstain from Sexual Sin:** "I urge you . . . to abstain from sinful desires, which wage war against your soul" *(1 Peter 2:11)*
- **Reminding to Love:** "Let us love one another, for love comes from God" *(1 John 4:7)*
- **Encouraging to Be on Guard:** "Since you have been forewarned, be on your guard" *(2 Peter 3:17)*

Clearly, Biblical *networking* is centered upon fostering *open and honest relationships,* which is another one of the six essential elements (the "O") of the PROVEN Path. It requires you to concentrate on *others*—instead of yourself, your rights, your expectations, and your circumstances.

By removing yourself from the center of the universe, you not only become useful in the lives of others, but also gain the "E" (an *eternal perspective*) that is similarly necessary for living out a PROVEN life. It's also an antidote for pride and leads to the "R" *(repentance)* and "V" *(victory)* of the PROVEN life.

Finally, the more you obey the commands of the Lord with a sense of purpose, you round out the *PROVEN* elements as you become more *passionate* about the Lord. In short, when you set limits upon what you're willing to do to obtain victory over lust by rejecting the "N" of *networking*, you're also rejecting the other letters and elements of your new title and role of a PROVEN Man.

■ MAKING THE DECISION

Right now, you may be facing a huge dilemma:

> ***If I don't take a networking partner, I won't experience lasting freedom, but if I share my struggles with another man, I may be judged or rejected.***

This fear is real. It's what keeps most Christian men suffering in silence. However, as you read in the verses earlier, God demands that our sins be exposed to light to be eradicated, and true *networking* is a primary method. That doesn't mean there won't be pain associated with the process. In fact, if one *networking* relationship doesn't work, find another. Freedom is not a one-shot deal, but a new and lasting Proven lifestyle. Accept that God is sovereign and will provide you with all the strength, determination, and support you need in every circumstance.

Don't let the devil try to rob you of your position by making you feel overwhelmed by the magnitude of the role and importance of *networking partners*. Rather, be thankful that the Lord is raising you up.

Remember, *networking* is not something you do alone. In fact, the Lord doesn't send men out alone, but two-by-two as fellow Proven Men. As you embrace *networking partnerships*, you'll be joining the brotherhood of Proven Men, which includes illustrious teams such as the 12 Disciples, David and Jonathan, Moses and Joshua, or Paul and Barnabas. It also includes everyday people, like myself and thousands of others, who are currently making the same decision to link up and not only go through the 12-Week Study but also share our lives with other Proven Men.

■ CHOOSING YOUR NETWORK PARTNER

Many ask what to look for in a *network partner* and where to find him. Following are a few suggestions.

First, there is no magical formula. Your *networking partner* simply needs to be someone who wants to keep growing closer to the Lord (*i.e.*, a fellow Proven Man). He doesn't necessarily need to struggle with the same sin.

Certainly, you should not eliminate a man merely because he isn't a spiritual giant. When I started Proven Men Ministries, I was not a pastor and had not attended seminary. What I had was freedom from sexual addiction and a hunger in my heart to help others break free.

I knew God had told me to form this ministry, but I felt a bit like the weeping prophet Jeremiah. I didn't think I could do this on my own and begged God to send me someone to journey with. Naturally, I waited with eager anticipation for God to send me someone like Billy Graham, because I wanted to reach a million men. So I asked the Lord to send me a spiritual giant.

One by one in my mind, I presented my choices to the Lord like the prophet Samuel who examined the strong sons of Jesse in Bethlehem.[1] Each time God said no. Then I looked at this 300 pound man named Brian who kept hanging around. He looked like a lost puppy, unsure of himself, but he kept sending me encouraging notes and wanting to spend time with me.

As Samuel first thought as he eyed the skinny young man David, I exclaimed "Surely not him, Lord?" as I viewed the opposite end of the extreme in Brian. But the Lord couldn't have made it clearer that I was judging as the world does, not seeing the heart of this giant with a tender spirit. I welcomed Brian into my life and began meeting weekly with him. I thought that I was going to train Brian, but it turned out that I was to experience a true *networking* relationship with him. Brian is now living in victory, the Vice-President of Proven Men, and my dearest ally and friend.

The Lord also brought me a pastor named Steve to mentor and guide me. Our three-way *networking partnership* is a sure foundation upon which we each face new hurdles and challenges, while sharing the victories and joys of life together.

I learned some valuable lessons about placing limits on who can be a good *network partner.* As you start this journey, be sure to grasp that a *network partner* is just that, a partner. Each man is a co-pilgrim, sharing similar goals and desiring the other to succeed. Both support, serve, and spur the other. As iron sharpens iron, so do two Proven Men sharpen each other *(Proverbs 27:17).*

As you seek a *network partner,* make sure that both of you are committed to being open and honest. One of the biggest problems many men face is a reluctance to be vulnerable with others. Therefore, you and your *networking partner* must be willing to push through the discomfort. Each of you needs to share intimate details regarding struggles, failures, hopes, dreams, and victories. This includes recognizing and then talking about feelings. Each must have the freedom and expectation to ask the other hard personal questions. Of course, confidences must be kept, because nothing breaks down a relationship faster than gossip and betrayal.

Finally, your primary *networking partner* must be a man, not be a girlfriend or your spouse. There are many reasons, including that you need to develop relationships with other men in order to foster a better relationship with your wife. In addition, it's damaging to a marriage to turn it into an accountability relationship, especially in the area of sexual sins. It often leads to a spouse engaging in a heightened, negative role of looking for and finding faults in order to point out every sin committed. It's also not necessarily in the best interest

1 1 Samuel 16.

of a spouse to know every minute detail of sexual sins, which can cause needless damage.[2] In short, you need a safe place to discuss struggles in a *network relationship* with another Proven Man.

■ FINDING A NETWORK PARTNER

It's your job to find a *network partner.* Although you are to pray for guidance, you must do the legwork. It can be someone you already know or you may have to diligently search for someone. Our website has additional resources for finding a *network partner* (See www.ProvenMen.org).

Although it may be beyond your comfort zone, the church is one of the best places to look for a *network partner.* One reason why the church is a great starting point is because it offers a variety of men's functions, such as men's prayer meetings, Bible studies, breakfasts, and church-sponsored sports activities. Those are terrific places to find another man like you that loves the Lord, but is stuck in some sin. They need you as much as you need them! If you're not regularly attending church, it may be time to start afresh. In fact, Christ called the church His bride *(Ephesians 5:25-32)* and we are told not to skip church just because it's not in vogue *(Hebrews 10:25).* A second great thing about the church is that they have male leaders who generally know of other men who desire a *network partner* and would be a good candidate. Take a risk and talk to your men's ministry leader or pastor for help.

In short, finding a *networking partner* requires that you take the initiative and not give up. It will be worth it because it will help you engage in open relationships and to network with other believers, which are essential components to living a Proven life. There is simply no replacement for personal interactions with other Proven Men.

■ MAKING THE DECISION TO NETWORK

Many, if not most men in the church, struggle with sexual purity in their relationships and in regard to pornography and masturbation. Most remain in bondage because they don't want to be the first to risk seeking out *networking partners.* Won't you break the mold, for your sake and that of the other men who need it as much as you do?

The prescription for lasting healing is to incorporate all six letters of a Proven life, which is completed by *networking* with other godly men. *Networking* is God's way of putting the

2 Included in our companion book, *A PROVEN Path to Sexual Integrity; Straightforward help with issues of lust, pornography, masturbation or other forms of sexual addiction from a Biblical perspective* is Appendix C, which addresses "What do I tell my Wife or Fiancée?". That article suggests an approach for first telling your girlfriend or wife of your struggles with sexual integrity.

final stamp upon you and freeing you from the false intimacy of lust, sexual affairs, pornography and masturbation.

Don't stop short of God's promises and power by going it alone or remaining isolated and closed. Choose today to take all steps necessary to link up with another man in an open and honest *networking partnership.*

■ USING THE 12-WEEK STUDY AS A FOUNDATION FOR NETWORKING

One of our key tools for helping men obtain sexual integrity is *The 12-Week Study to a PROVEN Path to Sexual Integrity.* Yet, it is a journey not meant to go alone. That's why we created a weekly meeting Guide (available for free on our website) for you to use with your *network partner* while working through the Study. First, you open your heart to change by daily completing the 12-Week Study. Second, you incorporate times of prayer for your *networking partner.* Third, you engage in weekly discussions with your *network partner* that also puts an end to secrets and shame by fostering openness and honesty—the vital elements of a Proven life.

Although not necessary, it's also helpful to read the companion book, *PROVEN Men: A PROVEN Path to Sexual Integrity,* because it outlines the basis of the Proven Path that includes networking.

For those wishing to be part of a weekly support group, we've also prepared a weekly Leader's Guide for support groups. Sometimes meeting in a support group leads to greater breakthroughs for many men. Others thrive meeting with another man using our free Guide for two men. Either way, you should not dismiss the importance of engaging weekly with a *network partner* while working through our intensive 12-Week Study. ■

For more information about Network Partners
or help becoming Proven in the area of sexual integrity,
visit our website at www.ProvenMen.org

Appendix B
Feelings Chart

 **Happy?** ecstatic? joyful? thankful? loved? loving? grateful? included? glad?	 **Sad?** disliked? unloved? grieving? sorry? regretful? miserable? remorseful? distrusted?	 **Confident?** respected? secure? safe? sure? capable? optimistic? appreciated? pleased?	 **Angry?** mad? hateful? bitter? upset? furious? outraged?	 **Depressed?** insulted? lonely? bored? withdrawn? excluded? incompetent? neglected? abandoned?
 **Stressed?** nervous? tense? negative? exhausted? debilitated? weary?	 **Indifferent?** unconcerned? weird? strange? foolish?	 **Afraid?** threatened? insecure? unsafe? paranoid?	 **Discouraged?** frustrated? exasperated? overwhelmed? defeated? disappointed?	 **Hurt?** betrayed? misled? resentful? cold?
 **Content?** peaceful? gratified?	 **Anxious?** worried? embarrassed?	 **Confused?** dismayed? unsure? perplexed? shocked?	 **Jealous?** envious?	 **Greedy?** selfish? arrogant? smug?

Made in the USA
Middletown, DE
10 April 2024

52838188R00033